TRAVELLING ON MY OWN ERRANDS

Travelling
on My Own Errands

Voices of Women from
The Mabinogi

Margaret Lloyd

Poems by Margaret Lloyd

For Bronwen,
So lovely to meet
you!. all the best,

Margaret
3-3-15

First published in 2017

ISBN: 978-1-84527-592-1

Cover design: Eleri Owen
Cover photo: Stela representing the Gallic goddess Epona, 3rd c. AD,
from Freyming (Moselle), France. Musée lorrain, Nancy; photo by Marsyas

Published with the financial support of the
Welsh Books Council.

Published by Gwasg Carreg Gwalch,
12 Iard yr Orsaf, Llanrwst, Wales LL26 0EH
tel: 01492 642031
email: books@carreg-gwalch.com
website: www.carreg-gwalch.com

I
John

Oet duis y cusil
'Profound was his counsel'

CONTENTS

PREFACE

The poems in *Travelling on My Own Errands* are written from the point of view of six female characters in the Four Branches of *The Mabinogi*. These Welsh mythological tales were first written down in the late 11th or early 12th century, though they often reflect an earlier time. The surviving manuscripts are from the 13th and 14th centuries. The poems in this collection strive to remain faithful to the general sweep of the external events in each branch. The inner voices and internal states and emotions of the women are sometimes expressed as the mind's voice which we are allowed to overhear, while at other times the women seem to be talking directly to us.

As convoluted and fantastical as are some of the events in *The Mabinogi*, I found that as I immersed myself in the tales, the women became flesh and blood. Their concerns, feelings, and challenges, their failures and triumphs, are highly engaging and often pertinent to a contemporary reader. Great mythic tales do not lose their resonance; they affirm that the past is present, now and here.

These poems do not limn the plots of the tales; rather they position the characters in moments during the unfolding of events. Each section is a poetic sequence of separate poems without titles. Epigraphs to each section taken from the text of *The Mabinogi* help orient the reader to the poems that follow. Readers wishing for more narrative context will find brief summaries of relevant sections at the end of the collection. These summaries are not necessary to the reading of the poems and, of course, they are no substitute for reading *The Mabinogi* itself, one of the finest wrought works of early European literature.

RHIANNON

Daughter of Hefeydd Hen

Part One

Eisted a wnaeth ar yr orssed. Ac wal y bydynt yn eisted, wynt a welynt gwreic ar uarch canwelw mawr aruchel, a gwisc eureit, llathreit, o bali amdanei, yn dyuot ar hyt y prifford a gerdei heb law yr orssed. Kerdet araf, guastat oed gan y march ar uryt y neb a'y guelei, ac yn dyuot y ogyuuch a'r orssed.

He sat on the mound. And as they were sitting, they could see a woman on a great tall pale white horse, with a shining golden garment of silk brocade about her, coming along the highway which went past the mound. Her horse had a slow, steady pace, in the mind of anyone who saw it, and it was coming alongside the mound.

I must be pursued at the right pace,
at the right time, and I must hear
a voice meant for me alone,

beyond the clamour of the world,
beyond laughter and concerns.
Riding through a night thick with mist,

I imagine entering your arms for the first time.
The strangeness of my life becoming real as I slowly,
methodically, cross into the world of sorrow,

the world all beings must live in.
I ride towards the threshold, the mound,
the gnarled oak trees and yellow grasses,

while the sparrows call in the night air.
I move toward the fires
and the murmur of voices.

I begin to feel the cold,
my heavy cloak. The mist lifts,
I see a line of stars.

I almost see you.

Almost seeing you is the same as not
seeing you, but my heart beats faster
and is impatient for your shape

and the right voice to summon me absolutely
into the present where I can say *yes*,
and begin to make plans like others

on the tenable earth. Yes,
there is confusion. Am I
the horse or the rider?

But then I feel my hands tug at the reins.

I am still and moving.
I am a secret riding down the road.

It is not obstinacy that drives me.

I know what I want
and what I don't want.

And let me remind myself–
the low-flying swifts with their pointed wings

are scavenging too.

Where do you think I am
while you are living your life,
occupied, carousing, conversing?

I am riding under the apple trees
whose fruit does not wither and the sun
does not change where it shines on the seas.

But I am ready, poised between who I was
and who I will be soon with you.

One man tries and then another, but the closer
they think they are, the further they drift.

It should be easy, as it suddenly is,
when you say the words that stay me.

I stop. It is all I want,
this moment that you too,
without knowing it,

have always been waiting for.

Why do we stop anywhere?
Our soul chooses.

Yes, I say when you finally speak.
I draw back my veil and look at you:

the man who will take my law into his own hands.
Behind your head I see Orion's belt

and an unending black beyond that.

Part Two

Hitheu Riannon a dyuynnwys attei athrawon a doethon. A gwedy bot yn degach genthi kymryt y phenyt nog ymdaeru a'r gwraged, y phenyt a gymerth.

Rhiannon herself summoned scholars and wise men to her, and after it seemed better to her to take her punishment than to quarrel with the women, she took her punishment.

The night is warm with a wind
from off the sea. In the courtyard

I want to be up against something–
stone, metal–or down against the ground.

Nowhere else to go. He
has to keep me steady. I want to be

pushed to the present
or back into myth,

or into his history, where there was
wine and dance, slow preparation

for a girl waiting for the right accusation.

In the morning he points out the swans
and their nine cygnets. We watch
their heads dipping and lifting,
feeding off the bottom together.

There is so much he does not want
given voice as though words
bring something into existence.

But I know what we do not say
becomes eternal.

And then does its work.

How can there be so much fear, so little trust?
This question stirs as I watch
the nightjars flutter in the oaks,

the shapes beyond shapes and a pale sky
beyond that. How can it be

that after giving birth in the night, I awake
childless, accused, and dishonored?

Who admires the birds?
Someone looking out a window?

Someone who has given up on all else?

There is sudden quiet and I think
the geese are gone.

But when I turn to look,
they are feeding in the grass

making a large silence. The river
coats my hands with mud.

I put them back in the water
to wash myself clean of it.

If birds live in a rainy country,
they can't help but get soaked

day after day. This is only over
the way the lives of gods on earth are over.

Small feathers float around me
as the flock of geese takes itself away.

I want to get past where I can't think–
into the wide sea beyond the waves

driven to reach the shore. But which shore?
Isn't there another one–in the Old North

where someone walks observing
what I observe this morning.
The sea and sky exactly the same colour.

It is all imagination.

This is not the real sea
throwing up its foam and hissing.

A run of mackerel and then whales
and dolphins came in. The winter
was warm until mid-January
and then the cold came.

And I am still without my boy,
a saddle on my back instead of under me.
Carrying rather than carried.

The mounting block becomes a kind of home–
as all places we live finally become,
no matter how shameful.

And isn't every story true?
In essence if not in detail?

We could all have bones thrown
across our breast for our responsibility.

It is rare to hold vigil against the hour of night
when myth breaks through and insists on its way.

After all, I have always been a story–

told first against the fear of night
and then to teach a lesson.

I have arrived to tell you all
there is some relief
from leaving off being
human and becoming
what runs in the fields
or sleeps in the stable,
eats grasses and carries
the burdens of the world.
It is a relief, I tell you.
The way shame releases us
from grandiosity, from showing
only pride. Let those who want
to take things away from you
have their way. Let people
who wish to save themselves
by using you, save themselves.
The truth is, I became more
than human, not less,
when I became the horse
carrying others on my back.

What gets returned, of course, is not the same
as what was taken away.

But I would rather see my son stride
with the moon over his shoulder
than a hoard of golden torques
or the dappled horses of Annwn.

After years of struggling to make what I have
be what I want,

I am not the same.

I leave my crown and mantle at the door
and walk into the room where you are.

BRANWEN

Daughter of Llŷr

'Y erchi Branwen uerch Lyr y doeth, ac os da genhyt ti, ef a uyn ymrwymaw Ynys y Kedeirn ac Iwerdon y gyt, ual y bydynt gadarnach.'

'He came to ask for Branwen daughter of Llŷr. And if it pleases you, he wishes to bind the Island of the Mighty and Ireland together, so they would be stronger.'

I cross from one great island to another,
the sun gold and later silver on the water.

Home smaller and smaller
stretched along the cliffs.

The sky full of white feathers.
Infinite space above me, below me.

You'd think I would have wanted
to be up on deck, my eyes open.

Instead, I sit below and sing
because I am afraid.

And when I arrive, I yield
to the god of generosity,

hoping each gift will make me a home–
ivory and jet, amber and gold.

And I give equally to the Travellers–
not just a glass of water or an old cloak,

a piece of coal, or peat–but topaz
and coral for protection,

knowing in my heart I am one of them.
All we see is scenery on the way to God.

Human life unfolds around strife–
that is the way shame works.

It is supposed to be over
but it never is.

Near the cairns the world has nothing in it
but thigh-high purple heather and yellow
tormentil close to the ground. We climb all day
from passage tomb to passage tomb
and see that the dead command the best view of all.
Now and then, the others drop from sight,
leaving me alone with the harsh wind
and the brown-horned sheep at the top of the world.
And for those moments, long or brief,
I feel the fear I felt before. If abandoned,
will I be remembered, tracked, found?

The punishment came soon enough,
made worse by loving a son.

The roiling kitchen, the blow
to my ears, the stench
of lamb's blood thick in the air.

I lived above myself, now I live below.
Here and there are small gifts.
I receive them gratefully. They come
from the mountain of the gods—
the gods who are not afraid
to exhibit themselves in all their folly.

I see the birds submitting
to the lack of seed in the harsh winter.
There is nothing and then nothing.

Is it a failure not to find what you want
in the place you should expect it?

Sometimes I think that what I want
is like God–God who is
so remote all I can do is worship.

But worship makes God larger.
And the larger God is, the harder to know.

If I stop worshipping,
if I stand on the bridge
with the swollen river running under me

without a prayer in my heart,
will God become less?

But how am I served by a lesser God?

I continue a strictness with myself–
not to prod the world into response.

We can scare the birds out of the nest,
but our hearts quicken when one suddenly

appears on the path of the morning–
a bird with a purple throat singing.

Quick, save me, I wrote, and sent it
to my brother under the starling's wing.

My eyes scan the horizon, to the north,
the south, and then more closely
along the line for any darker shapes
that signify my brother and his ships.
But the horizon is as empty as it is full,
and the gulls begin to sleep
with their heads on their sides.
The sea reflects nothing,
has no room for this lowering sky.
Yet suddenly, an arrival.
My brother and his men like black dragons
coming over the horizon to rescue me and fight,
fiercely singing as they row.

Standing on the bridge, watching
the still goose in the river
and two winter ducks swimming,
I give thanks.

I am almost thinking something,
the snow like the slow passage of time.

Later I place on the wall small stones
chosen near the water. Their markings,
all figures for thought–a cross,
a circle, lines like spears.

Is it permissible to be protected for a while?
Before the war, before my heart
will be broken either way?

Sometimes a man's heart is fierce, but not loyal.
He can't stop what he once started,
and wants to hear nothing but groans of dying men.

What is he signaling through the flames?
Through the breaking of the heart's cauldron
in one unending moment?

Perhaps there are things we can't get over.
Perhaps there are things we shouldn't.
Isn't this what the poets tell us?

I hear the raven cry three times
before it flies to find another carcass
over which to hunch its shoulders,
under which to find the soft decaying belly.
I am done with it. And I am undone.

Here is a confession that has no end:
we are dying and the last word
is like the last cup drunk while someone,
perhaps the one most loved,
perhaps the one who loves the most,
hurries out into the night.

I am wakened by goldfinch–
at least a hundred–
outside my window.
They are not quite yet the colour
they will be. And I know
I am not yet the colours
waiting for me. On the day
I don't have to be afraid
anymore, there will be no
goldfinch to hear and the stopping
of the clamour will not wake me.
No more assault. No pain,
no goldfinch, no light
or shade, just dark
that I can't even see,
on the day when I am not.

A feast always follows a sacrifice,
but how long can it last?

Death, do not leave me behind.

I cannot accept the consolation–
fire built by the sea at night,
singing of birds over the waters,
the companionship and history to come.

My heart is too full or too empty.
And now I know that death
is the place where too much
feeling and no feeling meet.

And now that it is over,
who will see me out?

Who will do something with my body
for the last time? Burn it or bury it.

Who will touch me while I am still warm
with my bereft and broken heart
on the green banks of the river Alaw.

CIGFA

Daughter of Gwyn Gohoyw son of
Gloyw Wallt Lydan
son of Casnar Wledig

Ac ual y bydant yn eisted yuelly, llyma dwrwf, a chan ueint y twrwf, llyma gawat o nywl yn dyuot hyt na chanhoed yr un ohonunt wy y gilid.

And as they were sitting thus, behold, a tumult, and with the extent of the tumult, behold, a mist settled so that not one of them could see the other.

Did I love too much? Or not
enough? Was I too kind?

Or too unkind? Did I imitate myself
until my self disappeared?

Did the same stories get told
until they cried themselves to sleep?

Did I look in one direction
too long? Or not long enough?

Did I arrive at the end
but keep walking until a hell

rose up and occupied earth?
When the mist settles over us,

I can see nothing but a cloud
swirling, competing,

never the same white, achieving
the complexity of life itself.

Yes and No the shifting colours
seem to say. No and Yes.

What direction will I
grope in now?

And when the mist lifts, the world
is empty, the fields

with no cows grazing, the halls
silent. Everything

once taken for granted,
now yearned for.

What can we do but seek
another way to thrive?

We live across the borders,
but only as outsiders.

I sit on the edge of our known world
with the wind running its mockery through me.

Every story has a minor figure–
a goad, a foil, a decoy. Or am I

simply here to provide the feasts?
Or am I becoming something else?

My body aches with the struggle
against all that seems below me.

I protest to save the present moment,
not having faith in tomorrow,

worrying what I can't control will destroy me.
But some winter evenings I simply watch

the low shadows of the birches in snow,
marks of the night birds, the clouds building.

When dawn appears, I sometimes sleep.

My husband returns
gently in my dreams,
breathing cold mist
rolling off the sea,
walking on Carningli,
hearing water rushing close
under the mounded grass.
He thinks of how
he can't get back
except in my dreams
where he can hear again
the close water and breathe
the mist from the bay
along the aching sea.

Do not give me news of the day.
I am still mourning
in the place where the grass
grows yellow and long.
Help me banish the world
that goes on without me.
Do not bring me news of life.
Do not bring me nightshade.
Bring me flax. Help me
burn quickly.

The god of temperance lives
in me like a black goat
caught in a rough thicket.
He does not see the blue lake
behind him and cannot reach
the grass. The sun
with its relentless democracy
will not leave him alone.
Where can I turn for help?
Tell me which god ravages constraint
like a lion mauling a young bull.

My story unravels somewhere
between two worlds,
touching the edges of both.

I lived in the small extremities
of my days. I had to go
where there is nothing and sit there.

I had to visit not-even-born-yet places.

Yes, the story arrives, beyond shame,
at its conclusion. I rejoice and feast.

But there is always another way to tell the tale.

GOEWIN

Daughter of Pebin of Dôl Bebin

Ac yn yr oes honno Math uab Mathonwy ny bydei uyw, namyn tra uei y deudroet ymlyc croth morwyn, onyt kynwryf ryuel a'y llesteirei. Sef oed yn uorwyn gyt ac ef, Goewin uerch Pebin o Dol Pebin yn Aruon… ac ynteu Giluaethwy uab Don a dodes y uryt ar y uorwyn, a'y charu hyt na wydat beth a wnay ymdanei.

And at that time Math son of Mathonwy could not live except while his feet were in the fold of a maiden's lap, unless the tumult of war prevented him… And Gilfaethwy son of Dôn set his mind on the maiden, and he loved her so that he did not know what to do about her.

I did not couple with some god,
I can tell you that. It was a human violence.
But I will never say all that happened
amongst those stolen sheets.

Is this the way it works?
First you want to own what you desire.
Then you want to destroy it.

That is what it takes
for you to walk away
erect, thriving, and free.

At first, I felt nothing.
And then I knew
I had always been alone–

Even when I looked out the window
of my father's house, protected
by a rowan tree and the red ochre
mined from the caves. Even
when I sat in front of the fire
drying my hair or lay
under the blanket singing
to myself at night.

Whatever safety, whatever
sanctuary I might have had,
was utterly contingent,

or never there at all.

Afterwards I lay in the bed, an unloved thing,
the rain falling from the trees, falling off the eaves,
rushing towards the sea with what seemed like
all the water in the world. The men returned
carrying the dead on their shoulders.

No one's feet to sit at or hold anymore,
I wandered behind the bell tower
with the four missing bells, into the quiet
of an old church. I lit a candle for the dead,
for the near dying, and for my maiden self.

I did not have the chance
to receive you as a guest
in the comfort of an evening,
to hang your coat upon the hook,
to offer you some drink,
to say *yes* and *yes*.

What has been entered has been entered,
and there is no compensation.

Let me remind you that even
exalted and given power,
you hear no more from me.

Though the howling in the night
will always sound like me
or, perhaps, like you.

Tonight restless winds scourge the town,
throwing the sea against the walls.
At noon under the grey rain, I stood
amongst the dead under their stones.
I want to believe there is a river
flowing up from the sea's ashes,
streaming through a good harbour
no wind touches, and into Dôl Bebin,
where a young girl runs shouting to her sisters,
the blue of her cloak flying behind her.

ARANRHOD

Daughter of Dôn

'Pa uab yssyd i'th ol di?' heb hi.
'Y mab hwnn, mab y ti yw,' heb ef.
'Oy a wr, ba doi arnat ti, uyg kywilydaw i, a dilyt uyg kywilyd,
a'y gadw yn gyhyt a hynn?'

'What boy is that behind you?' said she.
'This boy, he is your son,' he said.
'Alas, man! What has come over you to shame me, and to
pursue my shame, and to keep it as long as this?'

In my heart there is a figure walking
backwards one step at a time.

I lean forward to smell the sea,
but I know there are many seas.

In the country of a different sea,
perhaps I would want to speak of love,
but not in this one.

Half knowing has its uses. Half
saying can be a truth.

I turn and walk out the door
and then I walk for a long time–
rejecting consignment,
rejecting revelation.

Seeds have fallen and the skeletons
of weeds stand upright like sprigs
in a wedding or a funeral bouquet.

A white stag running through the trees,
the last leaves trying the wind. I arrive home
with pieces of abalone in my hand.

There is honesty to where I am,
torn between this and that,

this kind of pain I can bestow and bear
and that.

I am not owned as I turn
to one then the other.

There is news I don't want–
anything to do with heartlessness
or diminishment.

I know it is all out there,
and it all happened long ago.

Men are sleeping in their rooms.
They think they have to make a world,
dreaming while the rowan trees
winter in the early morning wind.

I am hoping, even now,
it can be undone.

I will sacrifice without limit–
even the back of my fair son walking away,
armed against the world.
I can only renounce him;
he can only leave me.
But it is his back I watch,
just as my eyes followed an oak leaf
down winter's cold water.
I stood by the river,
alone under the bridge,
registering absence when there was
nothing to be seen.
It is a life without comfort and rest.
I cannot abide an insult to my heart,
though his is the back I will watch
beyond where I can no longer see it.

I am not reliable in the way
others think I should be reliable.
I could easily keep walking
past where I usually turn around–
past fish heads, red dulse,
the smouldering fires.
I could enter the water,
walking through meadows of grass,
while the sun is falling under the sea.

I wind a silver chain around my wrist
near the pulse–to bind
what is already bound.
In the dim light of morning I wake.
And then I move.
This morning I protect
my knight with a pawn.
A mistake, perhaps, as it frees
the other knight.
There are choices we make
when the knot is too tight,
the heart too weary to calculate.

My brother speaks with equanimity.
He knows what is behind him,
and that he will find a way
to extract what he demands.

How do we live?
We disown ourselves; we disown each other.

But he will not find me on my knees.

My words are the eternal back of my hand.
My brother curses me; I curse the son I love.

I think most of us live
as though we were cast-offs
of the court, not even like the fool
who speaks his mind and plays
with a hundred words.
I struggle with the snow today
and how to disturb
this numbing beauty.

The goddess is tired of me. She is circling
the night sky and sends me nothing
but a mirror. I look at myself.
Behind my head is winter and the white
expanse leads to the woods.
She is unkind and I am unkind.
Will she give me more than just one pearl
each decade? Perhaps I'll stop waiting
and that will be that.
At least the mirror looks back.
But when my eyes slide away, winter stays
looking at me with its white gaze,
bleak and intent. It has no mercy.

The raw life of the heart has taken over,
with the sharp-beaked crows in the trees.
One flies with a large piece of flesh in its mouth.

The crows are not calling as they fly
from branch to branch. They are busy
making shapes against the purple sky.

I have moved to the highest room in my house,
closer to the tops of trees and the eyes of crows.

The moon sighs and asks nothing;
it is perfect as it is. I pray under it:

*O purple-black crow. Crow of the sky
and crow of the water. Many crows
swimming in the backwaters.*

But I have no offering for the gods–
not sound or light or any animal.

Not even my self.

The queen and the king
on a black and white board
stare straight ahead,
waiting to be moved.

I lean my head on my hand,
stroke my forehead slowly.
They say nothing can happen
until you give up.

Well, the audience is gone;
no one here to judge or insist.

If there is going to be a move,
move me.

BLODEUEDD

Part One

'A gwreic a geif ef ual kynt'... Ac yna y kymeryssant wy blodeu y deri, a blodeu y banadyl, a blodeu yr erwein, ac o'r rei hynny, asswynaw yr un uorwyn deccaf a thelediwaf a welas dyn eiroet.

'He shall get a wife nonetheless'... And then they took flowers of the oak and flowers of the broom and flowers of the meadow-sweet, and from those they produced by enchantment the fairest and most beautiful maiden a person ever saw.

I don't know how to enter life
because I don't know what life is.
I know what you think life is–
I could tell you exactly and at length.
But it doesn't help as I sit here
for the first time, looking out
at birds fluttering in the oaks,
meadowsweet blooming in the fields.
Why would anyone choose this?
For now, I want only the room,
the stone wall, silence.
This is my life, I say.
I have entered it.

The walls, too, want to make me
into something, and now I have largely
become that person, that wife. It is good to stray
outdoors on dirt paths, in the midst
of brush and bracken, the flowering broom
on the banks of the river, the river
that is going someplace.
The world teaches me new things
to want each day. The sun
finds the smallest blade to illuminate.
It might be that against time
I am waging war,
inevitably, hopelessly.

I know my heart is not the way it was;
it is not the way you made it.

You want to draw near, longing
for what my skin still holds.

But nothing summons me,
and it bewilders you.

When you look in the mirror,
you see yourself

and you see me watching.
But from where I sit,

I can't see myself–
only you,

and the grey wall and
the greyer ceiling.

You withhold and I withhold. And soon
there is a new world built of all that is
not said and shared–plans, triumphs, laughter,

indignities, and dreams–the castle
once built by revelation stops shining. Standing
in the field I watch the sun sink on the turrets

while the moon rises elsewhere, gauging,
measuring. But I am seized by love
with the flowers of late summer standing

and staring on either side–wild carrot,
white campion, the branching buttercup.
And all that I withhold from you is taken

by a stranger. This is the careless world
we have made. This, the careless night.

He and I hold the tips of our tongues
together, barely breathing,
a loud silence around us. Nothing
but our tongues
and our bodies behind our tongues.

How permanent is prohibition?
The absolute strictness
of one note following another on the scale?
The law of before and after.
Or is it the fly buzzing
inside the window until spring–
sometimes in such a frenzy it could destroy itself?

But there is enough mystery right here.
The blooming under my eyelids.
The mouth I want to enter
and the mouth I don't.

When he turned into a god
while I was kissing him,
I turned my head away. Later,
I told him what had happened.
He nodded as if I had pointed out
the colour of his eyes,
as if he knew desire exists
to be used any way we need to use it.

But when it's over, I thought to myself,
there will be silence, like after the birds
screamed outside my window in the dawn.
They woke me up then flew away, leaving
a silence in which I could
only hear you breathing.

I lie on my back, desperate
for him to enter me.
I don't know if I'm desperate
for the beginning or the end.
I am not used to such longing,
my head tossing from side to side,
as if desire can be shaken off.
But he keeps his steady eyes on mine,
and then without thought
I repeat the words *I'm sorry, I'm sorry.*
I am sorry for everything,
and I am talking to you.

I walk along the stone wall that divides
the forest from the forest.
There are wild apple trees here
and even the smallest apples are not bitter.
The earthnut at the base of the white plant
tastes dense and sweet, deeply made in the dark.
For some, who travel across the boundaries,
begging is a worthy way of life. Sweet fruit,
a bright piece of cloth, some water–
all who give get a blessing from the people
who have gone around the world.
I was blessed like that once and have not forgotten.
The perfect ferns in the forest point this way and that.
The heal-all stands in its certainty.
I am not afraid to be a beggar at his door.

Part Two

A'r nos honno y bu yr ymgynghor ganthunt pa furu y kehynt uot yg kyt. "Nyt oes gynghor it," heb ef, "onyt un; keissaw y ganthaw gwybot pa furu y del y angheu

And that night they took counsel together how they might be together. 'There is no counsel for you,' he said, 'but one: seek from him to learn how his death might come about.'

I have given up on all the birds
but the blackbird. That large
bird with a yellow beak
singing in the oak tree,
six notes and a final trill.
It has chosen me to know it
and its song is the only song
I hear, and I have to abide
by this one insistent life
and its demands.
Because I now bring
the blackbird into being
each morning at dawn,
its song forcing me
to dream of death,
to have my dream of love.

How quiet I became as we lay
in our wooden bed,
the rain dripping from the trees.

You felt me intent on something
and told me all I needed to know
to bring about your death,

as if you, too, had your own
dark dreams. Or can it be
you had no imagination?

Did something in you grasp
what was to come? Soon
you fell silent,

matching the silence with which I began.

In my desire for freedom,
a place to be myself,
have I created a prison?

Even the two white lilies
near the lake's edge begin to look
like prisoners–floating and beautiful

on the surface, their long stems
sinuous in the moving water,
but rooted in the shallows.

Whatever else is in me–soft
and subtle, an intimate perfume,
my eyes always the eyes of a young girl–

there is also a fierceness
that surprises me–nettles in the brush,
each one a capacity for deception.

I am curious about it.
All the urges on earth

are out there. All the shameful things
people can do to each other

are in the wind, floating
on the shifting waters,
hidden in the low marsh.

Any creation complies only so far,
and then can't be controlled.

Ask yourself–who cradled me
in their arms when I was small
and needed comfort? Who said

dear Blodeuedd and rocked me?
No one. All that happens,
happens without history.

Something is missing in me.
Or is something added? Or both?

I whisper to myself at night, I say
sweet white bones, sweet skin,
sweet love, dear Blodeuedd.

Perhaps the story should be repeated,
traced differently this time. But I say

let it unfold its joys and wounds again.
What gave me pleasure was hidden from myself–

hunted, longed for, despaired of,
but finally found. I am more afraid

and less afraid of lying alone
under the grey eaves, in the house of loss.

When you look into the night and see nothing,
I might be there. Any being, really,
can provide company, no matter how silent,

no matter how abject. It is presence,
and all too soon there will only be
a large absence. And I can never know

which spirits were invested in me,
yearning from the bottom of the lake,
dreaming in the cold, dank earth.

I was made as I was made,
but I became something else.

And then I was made again–
not for the light of day,
but for the margins and the night.

Was I made both times to make you?

When he is dead, do not place him
where no one will remember.
See that he has a stone somewhere.
Somewhere in a rough field,

where an owl's quiet flight
circles the centre of the earth.

NARRATIVE SUMMARIES

Rhiannon, Part I: Pwyll and his court go one evening to the magical mound of Gorsedd Arberth to see a wonder. A beautiful woman rides by on horseback. Three times someone is sent to find out who she is but can't catch up with her even though her horse is only walking. When Pwyll himself finally asks Rhiannon to stop, she does so and tells him that she has come hoping to marry him. Pwyll readily agrees and they set a time to marry.

Rhiannon, Part II: Three years after they marry, Rhiannon becomes pregnant. The night she gives birth, the midwives fall asleep and the child disappears. Out of fear, the midwives plot to accuse her of destroying her own child. Rhiannon accepts punishment rather than argue with the midwives. She is to sit by the horse mounting block for seven years and offer to carry guests and strangers to the court on her back. Eventually, her son is returned and her punishment ends.

Branwen: When Branwen, sister of the king of Britain, is married to the king of Ireland, her half-brother Efnisien feels insulted and in turn insults the Irish king. The king is well compensated, and Branwen is welcomed in Ireland for a time. However, the Irish courtiers cannot forget an insult to their king. After a year, Branwen is punished for that insult by being sent to work in the kitchen and is struck every day by the butcher. She sends a message to her brother who comes to Ireland with an army. War ensues and the Irish ask for peace and offer to make Branwen's son king of Ireland. Efnisien again feels slighted and thrusts the boy headlong into the fire, thus renewing the war. Almost everyone on both sides is killed. Branwen returns to Wales with the seven Welsh survivors and upon landing she dies of a broken heart.

Cigfa: Pryderi, who is married to Cigfa, offers the rule of his kingdom to Manawydan, who then marries Pryderi's mother Rhiannon. When the four of them ascend Gorsedd Arberth, a dense mist descends, and when it lifts, all signs of habitation have disappeared. The four survive by hunting and then working as craftsmen in England. When Pryderi and Rhiannon disappear into a mysterious fortress, Cigfa is left alone with Manawydan. Manawydan again becomes a craftsman and later takes up farming, and Cigfa becomes increasingly concerned about their loss of status. Ultimately, however, Manawydan's strange behavior turns out to be the key to securing the return of Pryderi and Rhiannon.

Goewin: Math, lord of Gwynedd, cannot survive without a virgin footholder, unless he is at war. When his nephew, Gilfaethwy, falls in love with the footholder, Goewin, the magician Gwydion foments war to separate Math from her. While Math is at war, Gilfaethwy rapes Goewin in Math's own bed. Goewin tells Math what has happened when he returns. He compensates her by marrying her.

Aranrhod: Math needs a new virgin footholder. He summons Aranrhod and to determine whether she is a virgin, he requires her to step across his magic staff. As she does so, she drops "a small something" and flees. Gwydion nurtures the child, who grows into a strong and beautiful boy. When Gwydion presents the boy to Aranhod, she feels shame and anger. She swears the boy will never have a name or arms, unless she gives them to him, or a wife "from the race now upon this earth." Through his magic, Gwydion tricks Aranrhod into naming and arming him, and the boy, Lleu Llaw Gyffes, grows into a man.

Blodeuedd, Parts 1 and 2: Gwydion and Math create a wife for Lleu out of flowers, and she is called Blodeuedd ('Flowers'). Blodeuedd, however, soon falls in love with Gronw, a neighboring lord, and together they plot to kill Lleu. They nearly succeed, but the plot ultimately fails, and Lleu kills Gronw. Blodeuedd is punished by being turned into an owl, a despised and nocturnal bird. Henceforth, she is called Blodeuwedd ('Flower-face'), a descriptive term for an owl.

ACKNOWLEDGEMENTS

Completion of *Travelling on My Own Errands* was aided by a fellowship to Hawthornden Castle International Retreat for Writers, Scotland, and by a sabbatical award from Springfield College. The first section of the Rhiannon sequence was published in *Envoi* 171 under the title 'Rhiannon Entering'.

I am deeply grateful to my family, the poets of Group 18, and my community of friends, artists, and scholars in Wales and in the United States for supporting me in this project— one which my life has been pointing towards for a long time. Many thanks, too, to Myrddin ap Dafydd, Eleri Owen, Dwynwen Williams and all at Gwasg Carreg Gwalch. My most profound debt is to John Bollard, my steadfast companion, for his important work on *The Mabinogi*, and for his critique and enthusiastic encouragement throughout the writing of these poems.

Margaret Lloyd was born in Liverpool, England, of Welsh parents and grew up in a Welsh community in Utica, New York. She received a PhD from the University of Leeds, England, and has published a book on William Carlos Williams' poem *Paterson*. *Travelling on My Own Errands* is her fourth collection of original poetry, following on *This Particular Earthly Scene* (Alice James Books), *A Moment in the Field: Voices from Arthurian Legend* (Plinth Books), and *Forged Light* (Open Field Press). A poet and painter, Lloyd lives in Florence, Massachusetts, and is Professor Emeritus at Springfield College, Massachusetts.